Unmasking The Strong Black Woman

16 Essays on How To Manage Your Emotional Health, Build Your Wealth, and Live a Juicy Life

The Frugal Feminista Presents: Unmasking The Strong Black Woman

Dear Frugal Feministas:

I can't tell you how happy I am sharing *Unmasking the Strong Black Woman: 16 Essays on How To Manage Your Emotional Health, Build Your Wealth, and Live a Juicy Life* with you. This body of essays comes from the hard lessons I learned from the not-so-happy nether regions of my soul.

And I know you can relate.

There are a lot of us brown girls walking around these streets thinking that the only way that we have permission to show up in this world is with a thick, tough exterior; the only right that we have in this world is to be the shoulder, the backbone, and the planted feet of our families, our communities, and our people.

We have been socialized to embrace the stoic, steely "Strong Black Woman" – the warrior princess that can hold it down, pull it together, and get it right for everyone, for everything, all the time, right this minute, without help and without struggle. You know that is complete and utter foolishness, right?

In my early twenties, I read bell hooks' seminal work *Ain't I Woman: Black Women and Feminism* and was immediately struck by one of her assertions.

What she wrote—without exaggeration—freed me. What she wrote put me on a journey of self-recovery and rescued me being a Strong Black Woman to being a black woman committed to living her full human experience.

To paraphrase, she wrote, strength is the ability to endure, but not overcome.

I repeat: strength is the ability to endure, but not overcome.

Let that marinate.

As sistergirls living with the benefits of social advances in mental health, technology and education at our disposal, I implore you to think bigger and happier – beyond the limits and walls of endurance. Remove what no longer serves you from your life. Attend to your self-care with precision and without apology—which is as much about how you take care of your body and spirit as it is about how you manage your money.

Just so you know, they will not be handing out awards or bonuses for suffering, martyrdom, or playing small, right before you die.

I created *Unmasking the Strong Black Woman: 16 Essays on How To Manage Your Emotional Health, Build Your Wealth, and Live a Juicy Life* as a testimony to playing big.

These sixteen essays are a compilation of two years of writing, reflection, and processing. Some pieces have been pulled from The Frugal Feminista site; I've written others just for myself, but have decided to share them with you here.

I've divided this book into three sections: Emotional Health & Juicy Living, Wealth, and Gentle Reminders for Recovering Strong Black Women.

It's my deep hope that reading this book will make you want to stand up for yourself, advocate for the life you want, and be demanding and relentless in your pursuit of it. I wish for you overwhelming and overflowing juiciness and happiness in your life— all day, every day, in the most mundane beautiful ways, and in the biggest fattest plumpest over-the-top ways.

Love,

"If I didn't define myself for myself, I would be crunched into other people's fantasies for me and eaten alive."

-Audre Lorde

Table of Contents

Emotional Health & Juicy Living

5 Feelings Every Black Woman Should Experience All Year

Every time a new year rolls around, it usually means that we start a discussion about the things that we want to do and want to accomplish. We break out the scissors and the glue and create beautiful vision boards with all of the people we want to meet, places we want to go, and things we want to purchase.

And don't get me wrong, I'm all for it. I still have my old vision boards from back in the day, which showcased my health and fitness goals.

But after some thought, I decided to flip the script. Instead of writing down and focusing on all of the things that I want to accomplish, I want to focus on all the ways that I want to **feel**.

Yes, feel.

If you are a black woman living in America, there are so many messages from our family circles and larger institutional structures that remind us that how we feel is not their concern when there is work to be done, food to be prepared, and problems to be solved. In other words, one of the societal expectations of black women is that we keep how we feel to ourselves. This is assuming that they even believe that we have a complex humanity that demands attention and cultivation.

It's up to us to make room for our feelings. And what that said, here are five feelings I'm making room for in my life...year in and year out.

the frugalfeminista
financial empowerment. girl power. juicy living

JOY: I want joy for you and for myself. But before you can relish in your joy, make sure you know what brings you joy. With a million and one things on your plate, have you ever sat down and took the time to figure what brings you joy? When I was a little girl, I used to think that joy was for other people and not for me. I was so busy being sad and miserable because my father wasn't around that I forgot that I was capable of such a positive emotion. This sense of sadness continued into my twenties until I sought support from a counselor. Talking about my past helped me declutter my thoughts so I could learn to enjoy my present and prep for a joyful future. I'm now well into my thirties and I know at least 10 things that bring me joy.

Here are some of them: sleep, reading, blogging, saving & investing, connecting with dope women of color online and offline, talking to my stoic uncle about sappy things so he can blush, harassing my mother and brothers, chilling with my husband, spiritual retreats and workshops, and a dollop of ratchet reality shows. (After you read this essay, brainstorm everything that brings you joy – the rachet and the righteous. Don't censor it. Make sure you schedule to do at least two of those things within the next week. Also, if you are looking for a good book on joy, I highly, highly recommend All the Joy that You Can Stand by Debrena Jackson Gandy. (I love her work.)

UNCONDITIONAL LOVE: We all need to feel that we have a home to which to return especially when we are not perfect, make mistakes, and are far from flawless. This home lives in the hearts and spirits of friends, our families, our online groups, our community organizations, and our religious and/or religious safe spaces.

the
frugalfeminista
financial empowerment. girl power. juicy living

Once I understood nugget, I freed myself of friendships that were hurtful and negative. Once free, I was able to be more intentional about giving the unconditional love and support to people in my circle that have always been there for me. Concretely this meant, I returned texts and emails in a timely fashion. I tried to say yes for invitations to come out and play and made it my business to create opportunities of celebration when I could.

CONFIDENCE: Confidence comes in so many shapes and forms, but at the core of confidence is being true to yourself and liking what you do and who you are. I know for me, a big piece of my confidence comes from knowing that I am a good saver and an avid reader and a life-long learner. If confidence comes to you through how you dress (and you're not going into debt for it), your culture, your friendships, or your art, make sure you give a lot of your attention to those things this year and every year.

DISCOMFORT: Did I just write "discomfort?" Yes, but not the physical or emotional kind that only brings stress, pain and sadness into your life. The kind of discomfort that I am talking about is eustress, which occurs when you step out of your comfort zone into your greatness. It's the kind of discomfort that precedes feelings of euphoria and optimism. It comes from finally writing your book, finally going back to school, finally making amends with a loved one, finally getting out of debt, or finally negotiating for a higher salary.

I know it sounds cliché, but time waits for no one. Seriously. Since you have but so much time to live out loud, make sure you are living it on your own terms, attending to your spirit and soul along the way.

the
frugalfeminista
financial empowerment. girl power. juicy living

10 Things That Every Happy Black Woman Knows

Are you happy? There is a happy black woman revolution happening! We are making decisions to get out of life everything we want: beautiful bodies, strong romantic relationships, healthy family connections, meaningful friendships, money, preferred careers, and grounded spirituality. We are doing it by monitoring how we think, what we believe, and how we act. Here are just a few of the things that happy black women know:

1. **EVERY WOMAN SHOULD HAVE HER OWN MONEY.** A man IS NOT a financial plan, no matter how much you love each other. (I can thank my favorite uncle, mom, and grandmother for that advice.)

2. **WHAT GOT YOU HERE WON'T NECESSARILY GET YOU THERE.** Some of the skills that we used to secure the positions that we currently have in our careers, such as technical skills, become less important as we continue on our career path. Since you have proven yourself to be competent and knowledgeable, it's the "softer" skills such as empathy, sense of humor, collaboration, and the ability to share and connect your personal story that get you remembered and included in higher profile projects and selected high-leverage opportunities.

3. **HAPPINESS IS A DECISION.** My childhood was not crazy, but I definitely had struggles—like many of us. For a long time, I allowed my circumstances to determine how I felt about myself and draw conclusions about the type of life I was destined to live. I carried that heaviness for a long time but realized in my mid-twenties that I had the power to redefine how I viewed the world. With that power, I chose to view setbacks as either opportunities or temporary.

the
frugalfeminista
financial empowerment. girl power. juicy living

4. **THE "STRONG BLACK WOMAN" DOES NOT EXIST.** As far as I am concerned, being strong for the sake of being strong is for the birds. And anyone that wants to affix that label to me can take that Superwoman cape and get on with the get on. No black woman is made of brick and no black woman will always have it all together. More importantly, they do not have to. Each black woman is entitled—despite what the media perpetuates—to embrace all of her humanity, the fragilities, the vulnerabilities, and the complexities. Period.

5. **WE ALL HAVE A TRIBE.** Some of us find our closest friends early on in life while others are late bloomers and are just getting to the groove of creating and sustaining meaningful friends. We all have a tribe. If you have not found yours yet, don't stop looking because they are looking for you, too.

6. **COURAGE IS A MUSCLE THAT CAN BE DEVELOPED.** I think Maya Angelou said something to this effect. You can build courage by being courageous at small things first like being the first to speak at a meeting or being the first to introduce yourself to someone that you want to get to know. Once you are comfortable with being courageous at small things you can be courageous at big things like quitting that damn 9-5 you hate, traveling alone, or relocating to a strange place to follow your passion.

7. **TRAVEL IS POWERFUL.** Travel gives you some of the biggest life lessons about culture, nature, and history. Travel also introduces a woman to herself because she is forced to step out of her comfort zone, deal with being different, and learn to connect with people in a short period of time.

8. **LIFE IS TO BE LIVED ON PURPOSE.** Life is way too short and before you know it, you may be collecting a Social Security check. In hindsight, most people regret the risks they did not take rather than the ones they did take. So, if you want to do that thing, whatever it is, take some action steps within the next 24 hours to get the ball rollin'.

the
frugalfeminista
financial empowerment. girl power. juicy living

9. **IT IS EMPOWERING TO ASK FOR EVERYTHING THAT YOU WANT 100% OF THE TIME.** Some of us engage in such debilitating self-talk that we talk ourselves out of pursuing an interest, asking a question, and taking a risk because we have already convinced ourselves that we will fail. This negative talk is irrational and has no grounding in reality. You cannot wait for someone to read your mind. You have to go out there and be proactive. While you may not get what you want all of the time, the practice of asking will become a habit and increase your chances of getting most of what you want.

10. **YOU HAVE THE RIGHT TO CHANGE YOUR MIND AT ANY TIME.** We make decisions with the information that we have at any given time. If more information shows that we should reconsider, slow down, or hightail it in the opposite direction, it's in our every right.

If you were ever like me and thought that happiness was for others, then let this essay be a gentle reminder that you are worthy, entitled, and built to be happy. Period.

Use your inner power and daily decisions to make time and space for your happiness.

To Be a Happy Black Woman. Now, That's a Radical Concept

It is almost blasphemous, but I will say it anyway. And if you want, I'ma make a t-shirt out of it. "I'd much rather be happy than be a credit to my race and gender." There. I said it.

Some say that's RADICAL. I say it's self-preservation and common sense.

Young black girls are raised and groomed to be ambitious, savvy, all-knowing, and all-doing caretakers, moneymakers, and beacons of service. We are taught that we have to lift as we climb— our men are depending on us, our children are depending on us, and the elderly are depending on us.

So what happens when all eyes are on you and so many place their lives into your hands? You take what was in your hands and put to the side to be in service to everyone but yourself. You let your life be led by others. Your self-concept gets wrapped up in how quickly and quietly you are able to please, problem-solve, and pamper.

I spent a lot of my time in high school and college living up to others' expectations of what a bright black girl should do and be; instead of realizing that what they wanted for my life and what I wanted for my life were two different things. And that my opinions TRUMP everyone else's.

the
frugalfeminista
financial empowerment. girl power. juicy living.

It took some time, but I packed up the black woman martyr/mother-of-the-earth suit, boots, and cape. In my life now, I don't need a costume or mask to languish behind or under. I arrive to situations as myself, not a representative.

I strive for connection to my humanity. I strive for happiness. I strive for connection to the people, activities, and things that bring me joy.

Ladies, How Full Is Your Abundance Tank? 3 Tips to Living The Life That You Want

Do you know of a woman that despite not-so-great circumstances keeps it positive and looks at the world through a lens of hope, faith, and overall positivity? They have confidence, stay calm, and know their purpose in life. Their light and energy are contagious and you just want to soak it all in.

If you answered yes, then you have come in contact with someone living life with abundance, which I define as an "at easeness" or "flow"— where who they are and what they do align and create possibility, confidence, and juiciness.

If you think about it in terms of a car, their abundance tanks are fueled by premium gas and are close-to-full, if not full.

Women living in abundance make it seem easy, but they achieve abundance because they make abundance a non-negotiable in their lives; they commit to it and work on their abundance every day.

If you are looking to increase the levels of abundance in your "abundance tank," consider the following:

1. **KNOW WHAT MAKES YOU HAPPY AND SCHEDULE TO DO IT.**

   Your most fulfilled friends tend to be the ones that are the most engaged—always involved in something. And it does not have to be Mother Teresa-worthy either! They are at Starbucks reading, traveling in some nation's backyard; they are at dinner; they are at the gym with a personal trainer.

   To be juicier, you have to do the same. Right now, think about five things that you have dreamed of doing; schedule to do the first on the list within 24 hours.

2. **PAY ATTENTION TO THE SIGNS OF A ½ AND ¼ ABUNDANCE TANK AND RESPOND ACCORDINGLY:**

   Signs that you are running low on abundance are very clear once you know what to look and listen out for. When you are not working with a full tank, you may find yourself doing a lot of the following:

   a. **SIPHONING THE ABUNDANCE OF OTHERS:** You may become demanding, needy, gossipy, and to put it lightly, far from a pleasure to be around. What you will see is that your friends with full tanks will pull away from you to preserve their limited amount and those with just as little, if not less than you, will create a low-vibration allegiance, where you all stuff your free time complaining, hating, and funkin' up your energy.

   b. **RECKLESS SELF-TALK AND DOUBT:** The gremlins of self-doubt, exaggeration, and paralysis begin to drown out your steady, calm voice of abundance. You begin to listen to these voices that tell you that your pursuit of happiness, in whatever form it is, is not for you because you are too young, fat, old, unworthy, dumb, black, inexperienced, etc.

the frugalfeminista
financial empowerment. girl power. juicy living

c. **YOU SPEND ON THINGS THAT YOU DON'T NEED OR WANT:** Impulse spending and chronic shopping are signs that you are trying to fill a void. Shopping also provides a momentary sense of power and control. It provides fleeting purpose and calm, which if not replaced with meaningful acts of abundance, creates serious consequences, both emotional and financial.

d. **YOU MAY EVEN MINDLESSLY EAT TO KEEP YOURSELF SUPERFICIALLY ENGAGED.** Like shopping without a reason, mindless eating provides temporary satisfaction. But at the bottom of this type of eating, there is a desire for distraction and escape.

3. **COMMIT TO KEEPING YOUR ABUNDANCE TANK AT LEAST ¾ FULL AT ALL TIMES.**

   As they say, prevention is better than cure; the same principle applies when you are being deliberate about keeping your abundance tank full.

   a. **STAY ENGAGED.** Keep yourself engaged in at least two activities that you love all of the time: One of the easiest ways to ensure engagement is to hang out with cool, abundant people.

   b. **DEVISE SOME STRATEGIES TO HANDLE THE 50 PERCENTERS.** This may be hard if you really care for the 50%er in your lives. But there is no point in both of you living below capacity. Ask them to engage in some self-reflection to uncover what they enjoy doing and point them in the direction of a resource.

If they are not solution-oriented at this point in their lives, it is ok to limit communication with them. If you had lunch often, be prepared to be busy, send out texts instead of phone calls of encouragement; don't meet them alone, bring your more abundant friends.

Abundance is your birthright, ladies. Don't forget!

6 Signs That You Are In Need of a Mental Health Day

I first heard the term "Mental Health Day" my junior year in college. Coming up the stairs from an afternoon class, I saw one of my dormmates in her jammies sitting on the step.

"Are you okay?" I asked.

"Yes, I just needed to take a M.H.D.?" she replied.

"A what?" I asked.

" 'A Mental Health Day'. I was just feeling so overwhelmed with papers and finals that I just needed to take a day off." she explained.

Back in college, I still suffered from The Black Women Superhero Syndrome so I was quick to dismiss Christine as whiny and privileged. But NOT now. Since I done boxed up that cape, them boots, and them tights, I feel no guilt, shame or indignation for engaging in mental self-care and neither should you.

Here are a few signs that you are in need of a M.H.D.

1.YOU ARE IRRITABLE: You snap at everything; I mean everything: it's too hot; it's too cold; everybody is breathing too hard; everyone is smiling too widely. Maybe you need to take the day and go to a park, a mindless movie, or a kickboxing class.

the
frugalfeminista
financial empowerment. girl power. juicy living

2.YOU ARE LOSING AND MISPLACING THINGS: Glasses, keys, wallet, shoes, or anything else that you regularly use. This means that you are moving way too fast. You probably wake up feeling that you are twenty minutes behind schedule. Perhaps a nice lazy day in front of the television picking lint out of your belly button will slow things down enough for you to feel that you have regained control over your life.

3.YOU SPEAK INCOHERENTLY: Incoherence takes two forms. You start a sentence, but never complete it. On the other hand, you start a sentence and never stop talking or get to the point. With both forms, you may be speaking really, really fast or really, really slowly. Both reveal that you are running low on sleep and energy and need to focus. Take a day of sleep, prayer, and meditation to get yourself centered.

4.YOU ARE LOSING INTEREST IN GROOMING: Taking a showering, running a comb through your hair or a toothbrush across those teeth becomes a chore and a burden, so you stop attending to your hygiene. Maybe instead of going out into the world like this, take a day or two to relax and recover from having to be responsible and on-point all the time.

5.YOU ARE SPENDING A LOT OF MONEY WITHOUT REASON: When you are pressed to the hilt, you may resort to shopping to relieve your stress. The more stress you have, the more outlandishand extravagant your purchases become. Try taking a day to luxuriate at home with a spa treatment.

6.YOU HAVE SEVERE CRYING EPISODES: If you have been ignoring these emotions by doing "business as usual," believe me, you are headed for a breakdown. Take control of your emotional health by taking the time to speak to someone about what is going on. It could be a professional, a spiritual leader, or someone that you can trust.

Attending to your mental health is no joke and taking M.H.D's on a regular basis is an easy and effective strategy that will keep you centered and sane.

You are your own first doctor.

How I Use Living Social to Help Me Deal With My Seasonal Depression

I am not sure about you, but I get a major case of the sads during the winter. One Sunday, I was watching Akeelah and the Bee and found myself bawling—deep belly tears. And I couldn't stop myself.

I didn't understand why I was crying, but luckily I've learned that part of my journey as a browngirl trying to make sense of this world is that I don't always have to have the answers; I've also learned that asking questions isn't always helpful.

Sometimes all my spirit needs from my intellect is space and acceptance.

Well, in the middle of the last New York City snowstorm, where I was locked in my house for two days on my second bout of uncontrollable crying, I heard a small voice say, "Chick, you're not gonna make it. You need something. You are fading."

Right there, I went to Living Social and searched for an escape. After a few minutes, I found one.

I pulled out my credit card and booked a trip to The Bahamas: four days, three nights, airfare, and hotel. It cost $549 with taxes included.

the
frugalfeminista
financial empowerment. girl power. juicy living

Though I was privy to this strategy (stashing cash for emotional emergencies) for close to nine years, 2015 was the first year my seasonal depression got so bad that I needed to get away.

During one of our many sessions, my mentor and counselor Mrs. P. told me that she kept a carry-on packed for weekends when she needed to get the hell out of the City. Her particular destination wasn't The Bahamas, but it was Puerto Rico for the weekend.

Booking a flight to The Bahamas for me was far from an impulse. My spirit was responding to the emotional emergency that was occurring in my soul.

As a personal finance coach, I encourage my black girl clients to stash away money for emergencies like these, so they can swiftly respond to what Mama Oprah likes to call the whispers in their lives, without going into debt and feeling guilty.

If you know yourself well enough to know that you may need a getaway to help ward off seasonal blues, begin with as little as twenty dollars a week.

You won't regret it.

the frugalfeminista
financial empowerment. grl power. juicy living

4 Signs You Know It's Time to Let a Friendship Go

I have a tendency to hold on to friendships longer than I should because I am loyal and often worry that I may hurt their feelings if I begin to pull away.

Can you relate?

But the one thing that growing up has taught me is that life is about phases, changes, and breakthroughs. You can't (and must not) be afraid to respond to the whispers and the writing on the wall when it is time to move folk from the friendship zone to the holding cage of friendly strangers and acquaintances.

Here are four signs that it's time to part ways with some of the people that you call "friend".

1.WHEN YOU SEE THAT THEY ARE CALLING, YOU LET IT GO TO VOICEMAIL: That is your intuition speaking to you. You let it go to voicemail because when you see their name on the caller ID, you have a visceral response. And basically, you want to avoid pain— which you subconsciously envision when having to be fake, guarded, and full of pretense once you decide to speak.

the
frugalfeminista
financial empowerment. girl power. juicy living

2.IF YOU DON'T CALL, THEN THEY DON'T REACH OUT TO YOU.
Another sign that you need to let a friendship go is if you are doing all of the heavy emotional lifting of the friendship. If months go by and you don't hear from your friend, unless they want your advice or for you to solve one of their problems, then it is safe to say that you should start cutting them loose from your VIP friendship roster. They obviously are not making the cut.

3.YOU BOTH PLAN TO MEET, BUT NEVER DO. This is the "all talk, no action" friendship. You love texting or saying "Girl, so when are we going to get together?" But when it comes to pinning down a date, there is absolute radio silence on the other end. I get it. We are all busy with our respective lives and that is okay. Just don't say that you are good friends. Call it what it is— you are texting buddies and if staying in touch and communication requires more than pressing "send," then it is not going to happen.

4.THEY FEEL THREATENED BY YOUR ACCOMPLISHMENTS. I have had a few (former) friends who would literally change the subject when I was in the middle of sharing my success on a particular passionate project or an obstacle I had been able to overcome. They threw this shade despite the hours of cheerleading and support that I genuinely gave to their shine. If you have haters cloaked in friends' clothing, protect your heart and run in the other direction, because their intentions are completely in favor of your failure.

If you feel like Mase from that InstaPurge fiasco on Instragram and fear that you will only have a few friends when you cut through the clutter, don't forget this nugget: you don't need a lot of friends, you just need good friends. And those are few and hard to come by. My mother-in-law always says, "If you can count the number of true friends that you have on one hand, then you can consider yourself blessed."

Wealth

the frugalfeminista
financial empowerment. girl power. juicy living

Are Black Women Building Wealth in Their Community?

A few months ago, I had the opportunity to view a film called "Black Heirlooms. " It chronicles the financial and emotional impact that a lack of proper estate planning has had on one African- American family's legacy of love and community.

Watching the short documentary was so moving that it inspired me to speak to my 74 year-old mother about her affairs. Luckily, I learned that she is set in terms of a drafted and updated will, her plot is paid for, and she showed me where she has put the important paperwork.

I did not ask about my father because I did not grow up with him, although I know where he lives. It will take a lot of emotional strength for me to do this but I promised myself that I would pick up the phone this week and call Antigua to see what's up with his affairs and what role, if any, I am supposed to play in handling his final wishes.

But my reality is not uncommon: black children being raised by single-moms. So, when the discussion about how families can ensure that wealth is organized and passed down to the next generation, I look to black women to serve as a central part of the equation.

African-American women are the financial pillars of their families, whether they like it or not, whether they plan for it or not. According to a 2013 Prudential Financial study called "The African-American Financial Experience," compared to women overall, African-American women are significantly more likely to be decision makers of their households.

Also, African-American women, compared to other groups, are more likely to carry the financial responsibilities of the household on a single income and head more multi-generational households. So, how can Black women take the lead in closing the wealth gap in our community? I think we can start from the beginning— by starting to have conversations about the inevitable interplay of death, family, property, and wealth in our community sooner rather than later and filling in the gaps in our own financial acumen.

So, this week, schedule a Saturday afternoon to:

‣ Sign-up for a class that teaches about estate planning, financial self-awareness, and the importance of intergenerational wealth;

‣ Make sure you have taken care of your financial basics: emergency fund, retirement, and eliminated debt. If not, set plans in place to lay this financial foundation;

‣ Update your beneficiaries;

‣ Speak to your spouse (or begin the process yourself) about organizing files;

‣ Read up on living trusts or wills via the internet or a book from the library;

‣ Get comfortable with the fact that we all are going to die, so preparing for it will make the grieving process easier for those loved ones who are left behind;

‣ Contact an estate planning attorney to discuss first steps;

‣ Speak with your elders about the state of their affairs.

Promise yourself that you will get started ASAP on this list.

5 Things Your Financial Frenemy Will Say to Keep You In Debt

When you decide to pull-up your big girl panties and take charge of your finances like a grown woman, you may begin to realize that everyone will not be happy with your new frugal and fabulous lifestyle.

Your shopaholic friends will become your new financial frenemies and say things to keep you chained to the door of revolving credit, conspicuous consumption, and living beyond your means.

But they will never outwardly admit that they want what's financially worse for you. Because they are like wolves in sheeps' clothing, they will pretty up what they have to say—the way a true financial enemy would do—with flattery and platitudes.

Here are five things that financial frenemies love to say to appeal to keep your financial situation in critical condition:

1. YOU ONLY LIVE ONCE (YOLO): It's true; you only live once, but here is something else to remember: each of your credit card bills, mortgage payments, and car note has their own life cycle OAM (Once A Month.)

2. "BUT IT IS ON SALE…" If you are desperately trying to adhere to a budget, a financial frenemy will gladly try to throw you off your course to debt-free living by saying, "but it's on sale" to justify something that is not scheduled in your budget. What your financial frenemy fails to understand is that buying unnecessary items whether for a little or a lot is wasted money if it is not a need.

the frugalfeminista
financial empowerment. girl power. juicy living

3. "YOU WORK HARD, YOU DESERVE IT." This statement really kills me. When your financial frenemy starts whispering this yiddy-yadda, ask them to be more specific about what "it" really means. Because when it comes to spending money that you do not have on things that you already own, "it" really means the following: less money, more debt, more crap, and more clutter. I doubt that that is something you worked hard for or deserve.

4. "IT'S AN INVESTMENT..." Your financial frenemy really has a warped understanding of the definition of "investment" when she views spending your tax refund or rent on clothes, hair, electronics, or a car—all items that lose value over time.

Quick reminder, as one of my financial-friends-in-my-head Michelle Singletary loves to say, "If it is on your ass, then it is not an asset."

5. "BUT THAT'S WHAT CREDIT CARDS ARE FOR..." Your financial frenemy will say this when she is trying to convince you to buy something that is WAY out of your financial comfort zone. I mean, way out. Here's the thing: credit card money IS NOT yours. If you could not afford to buy an item without the credit card, how do you expect to repay that amount of money PLUS the interest that is slapped on for borrowing someone else's money?

Discerning between you financial frenemy and financial friend is a cornerstone to developing a healthy financial backbone. But be strong and of good courage when you come across the forked tongue of your financial frenemy. Your wallet and your financial future depend on it.

the
frugalfeminista
financial empowerment. girl power. juicy living

Money CAN Buy Happiness

We live in an extreme society. One where we can find the morbidly obese and the fatally thin, both by personal choice and volition. A society where there are those who work eighty hours a week while there are those who refuse to work. A society of ultraconservatives and "bleeding-heart" liberals.

With such a polarized society, it's not a shock to find the discussion about the relationship of money and happiness as equally dichotomous and mutually-exclusive. To some, money does not create happiness; in fact, it is the source of evil. On the opposite side of the spectrum, we have those who worship money, elevating it to a status of omnipotence and employing all means to make more of it.

Money and happiness.

Those elusive powers and agents. We expend most of our adult lives in search of an abundance of both, one often at the expense of the other. A holistic approach to understanding their relationship and striving for both, then, is in order to strengthen and sustain our financial and spiritual lives.

the
frugalfeminista
financial empowerment. girl power. juicy living

Those who claim that money causes or creates problems and that it has no bearing on contentment and self-actualization need to take a more thoughtful look at the face of poverty within this country and outside of its borders. Money can buy happiness in the sense that it grants options and a voice to those barred from participating in the most basic human experience which, at a minimum, includes health, education, safety, and life purpose.

Once these fundamental needs are met, an increase in money begins to take on diminishing returns because of our human capacity to adapt to our environment. This means two things. First, we get easily bored once we have grown accustomed to a new comfort, whether it be a new car, a new tummy and nose, vacation-home, or handbag. Secondly and equally important, we keep looking upwards and around at what the next level up has to offer.

Newer. Shinier. Faster. Bigger. Sexier.

This cycle of using money to make purchases of increasingly more exotic, extreme, and intense locations and experiences in hopes of attaining a sliver of happiness is what behavioral economist coin, "the hedonistic treadmill".

And getting off of this treadmill is hard largely because Americans have been conditioned through overexposure to big business media, not to think for themselves. Not thinking for yourself leads you to value the opinions of others more than your own. Not thinking for yourself, additionally, puts you at odds with your authentic self and your personal truth.

the frugalfeminista
financial empowerment. girl power. juicy living

How many times have you been aware or noticed the following pattern? You are excited about the purchase of a particular item, fantasize about how it will complete your look, how important and sexy you will feel when you wear it or own it on your way to the counter or sales manager. You buy it. You're elated. You wear it and/or use it a couple of times. Weeks pass by and you are not as excited about that same item that produced such an intense sense of satisfaction as you were before. So, you go shopping, looking, and hoping for something new to catch your eye to make you feel important, alive, and centered again.

Intuition would lead you to conclude, then, that shopping and buying a lot of different stuff is not going to fill that void, that thirst, and that want to be fully present. EVER. Yet, you continue to do it because you somehow trust the fantasy of television more than you do your own gut. You would prefer to feel that something is wrong with you (rather than the marketing tricks and lies) and perhaps you are not buying the right item or enough of it to bring you joy, so you venture to consume more excessively and deliberately.

Stop This Treadmill! I Want to Get Off

Finding happiness with your money begins with first finding peace with yourself. This is not a call to throw away all of your worldly possessions or a campaign to isolate yourself from the conveniences of modern society. What it is, however, is an appeal for you to reflect and unearth your values, interests, likes, and wants. Once you have uncovered who you are, you can then use your money to fund, enhance, and nurture these experiences. Below is an example of my interest and how much (or little) money I need to make me feel happy.

SEVEN THINGS THAT MAKE ME HAPPY & THE COST

‣ Pedicure: $ 18 every three weeks

‣ Brunch with girlfriends: once a month $15-$20

‣ Long walks: Free

‣ Travel: anywhere between $200 a weekend trip to DC $1,000 to attend carnival in Antigua

‣ A good lecture or networking event: free-$30

‣ A clean bathroom: $10 (cleaning products)

‣ Personal tantric yoga retreat: $300

Now it's your turn: Please take 15 minutes to make your list. Perhaps you'll be surprised to discover that it may be the nature of your spending rather than the amount that you spend that is the source of your discontent or bliss.

8 Ways That Black Women Can Improve Their Relationship With Money This Weekend

Growing up in a household led by a single-mother who immigrated from the Caribbean and was partly responsible for supporting some of her siblings make their way to the United States, I saw firsthand how her role as Chief Financial Leader (CFL) and Head Emotional Caretaker (HEC) left my mother emotionally burnt out, overwhelmed, and financially depleted.

I think part of the work in our sister circles, community organizations, Black think tanks and churches is to discuss or explore how African-American women can better navigate the emotional and financial implications of these roles. They can be draining at least, and devastating at worst, especially those who are ill-equipped and unprepared to handle the magnitude of these responsibilities.

In an effort to bring more financial control and emotional support to all of the African-American women, I think we should start with small and deliberate acts of financial self-care. In fact, I believe every black woman should host their own Financial Self-Care Weekend.

A Financial Self-Care Weekend is an important first step in giving black women the space to organize their thoughts, emotions, and finances so that they can be there for themselves and others in their lives. With a Financial Self-Care Weekend, time gets to stop so black women can focus on themselves: attend to their spirits, create long-term and short-term financial goals, and create action plans to actualize them.

Here is an example of what you can do to prepare for and benefit from your first Financial Self-Care Weekend.

1. ANNOUNCE IT. In preparation for this weekend, tell everyone that you know that you will not be available for socializing. If you have kids, find a way to have them go to a family member's house so you can get some time to yourself. If you are married, let your husband know that you are off-duty for the weekend. (At a different time, the two of you can do a couple's financial retreat.)

2. CREATE AN ABUNDANCE AND PROSPERITY SOUNDTRACK: Find as many songs as you can to inspire you and encourage you to attend to your emotional and financial worlds. I love "Strength, Courage, & Wisdom," "Ain't Nothing Going On But the Rent," "Happy," "A Rose is Still a Rose," "Beautiful", and "Empire State of Mind."

3. PREPARE FOR A POSITIVE EXPERIENCE. Buy healthy snacks ahead of time and make your space beautiful and clean, so you can make the Financial Self-Care Weekend a sensually positive experience.

4. USE MEDIA TO MAKE YOUR MONEY GROW. Identify a range of movies, films, and documentaries that will soothe your soul, entertain you, and deepen your understanding about the importance of financial literacy and wealth building in your family. While I can't speak for your personal tastes in movies, I know that *Keeping Up With the Joneses* and *Confessions of a Shopaholic* are films with strong themes around financial literacy and consumerism. They are also somewhat entertaining. On the other hand, documentaries that will raise your consciousness level about the wealth game include: *Spent: Looking For Change* (narrated by Tyler Perry), *Black Heirlooms*, and *Maxed Out*.

5. REFLECT ON YOUR FINANCIAL IDENTITY. Think about your current financial identity. Are you a money hoarder, a spender, or somewhere in between? Think about how and why this identity formed and if it benefits your future self to continue relating to money in this way.

6. ORGANIZE YOUR FILES. Take the first step to putting structures in place around budgeting, downsizing the number of credit cards that you use, and setting up appointments with your bank and workplace to better educate yourself on retirement options and policies.

7. ACT AND AUTOMATE: While automation is not the cure-all for building a strong financial foundation, it definitely is an excellent tool. Over the weekend, automate the amount of money that you want to save every pay period from your checks. The rule of thumb is that you should aim at saving 20% of your take-home pay all of the time. Set your account to swoop in and remove 10% each time before you can even miss it. An online savings account like Capital One 360 and Ally are great places to start and have above average interest rates for savings accounts. If you can't swing 20%, start with 5% or even 2%. The most important thing is that you start now and stay consistent.

8.REPEAT AND REFINE: You can't completely overhaul your finances in one weekend, but you can make them a lot better within 48 hours. Once you start the process of reconnecting with your finances, you will get a better gauge of what your financial next steps will be. This is the essence of repeating and refining: your second Financial Self-Care Weekend will take its cue from the first, in the same way that your 22nd Financial Self-Care Weekend will be an extension of all that came before it. You will see that as you make more progress with your finances, your Financial Self-Care Weekends will be about making tweaks, adjustments, and pivots, instead of major reconstructions.

The most important part of making sure that our family's finances are taken care of is, to ensure that the woman holding the purse strings has the time and space to take care of herself financially and emotionally. No?

10 Best Book Picks for Black Women to Read About Self-Love, Money, and Career

I love books. Seriously.

Despite all of the things that pull my attention on any given day, I make it my business to DEAR (Drop Everything And Read) at least twice a day. I get my reading fix in during my hour commute to work and my hour and fifteen minutes commute from work.

What I learned about myself is that books are a major part of my self-care ritual and a fundamental way of how I relate to the world. It is also how I show my love, care, and concern for my fellow sistergirl. If you speak to me, you will always leave with at least two book recommendations.

So here are ten of my favorite picks:

Girl, Get Your Money Straight.
Glinda Bridgforth.
http://amzn.to/1ybJ3qS

I had the opportunity to meet Mrs. Bridgforth when I was in Detroit. I acted the same way a Beyoncé fan would have carried on when I saw her. This book and her other books changed how I saw money and how I viewed wealth. This book started me on a financial self-awareness journey. I eliminated all $65K worth of debt, started The Frugal Feminista, and made wealth a priority for my family and me.

The One-Week Budget.
Tiffany "Budgetnista"Aliche.
http://amzn.to/1DHNTOF

Tiffany is like my sister from another mother. If you are a baby to budgeting, then this book is for you. Tiffany assumes nothing about your financial acumen, which is a great thing if you need the fundamentals of budgeting laid out for you. The tone of the book is super conversational, so you feel like Tiffany is sitting right next to you at the kitchen table. Plus it's a #1 Amazon best-seller. There's a reason for that.

the frugalfeminista
financial empowerment. girl power. juicy living.

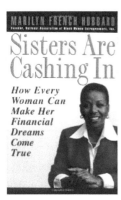

Sisters Are Cashing In: How Every Woman Can Make Her Financial Dreams Come True.
Marilyn French Hubbard.
http://amzn.to/1N5jBtD

This book isn't about worksheets or ratios to make you rich. Marilyn really explores the concept of wealth in a holistic way. This book delves deeply into tapping into your potential. She gives strategies on how to break away from negative thinking, beliefs, and influences to get you closer to the life that you want.

Sistergirl Devotions: Keeping Jesus in the Mix on the Job.
Carol Mackey.
http://amzn.to/1O59y4V

I met Carol at an Association of African-American Women in Higher Education event. As the former editor-in-chief of Black Expressions Book Club, she shared her knowledge about the shifts in the publishing industry of black authors. In addition to all of the nuggets that she shared, I bought her book at the event. Carol is a devout Christian and the intended audience is African-American Christian women. I think, however, that the 90 devotions can help any sistergirl along any spiritual journey make the most out of the concrete jungle that often is the workplace. One of my favorite quotes is, "It is my belief that people who like to make others' lives miserable are spiritually bankrupt. Their lives are so joyless and unfulfilled that they use their jobs as a substitute to satisfy the emptiness." Can I get an amen?

Interaction to Transaction: How to Get Comfortable When Asking for the Sale.
Nancy Roberts.
http://amzn.to/1O59y4V

I came across this sale gem at the Get Radical Conference. This was when I started thinking about venturing into coaching but was having some serious blocks about asking for the sale from my Frugal Feminista community.

In a one-on-one session with Nancy, I realized that my inability to promote my services was because I had major problems with receiving money and asking for money as opposed to saving money, making money, or giving money. This book is part money, part entrepreneurship, and all mindset targeting women with a problem asking for what they want and placing value on what they deserve.

Self-Love, Self-Esteem, Self-Care

The Sacred Bombshell Handbook of Self Love
Abiola Abrams
http://amzn.to/1Fdinly

This book is everything. From the first pages where she shares what caused the demise of her two-year marriage, the self-doubt and damage that it caused to her self- esteem, to all of the probing questions and emotional exercises that she forces readers to do to become their own damn bombshells in 11 areas of their lives, this book guides you into uncovering your best self.

Black Female Vegans Speak on Food, Identity, Health, and Society.
Breeze Harper. Sistah Vegan.
http://amzn.to/1PhtYJj

If you have been thinking about the role that diet plays on your well-being as woman of color in this society, this book will BLOW.YOUR.MIND. This book had me reeling and ever-so-conscious about my eating habits and thoughtful about my relationship with food, but meat in particular. Even if you never decide to be a full-blown vegan, this book will make you think more deeply about your food habits, the environment, and the role that institutional racism plays in your food choices. Extremely powerful.

How Did I Get So Busy? The 28-Day Plan to Free Your Time, Reclaim Your Schedule, and Reconnect with What Matters Most.
Valorie Burton.
http://amzn.to/1FdiYtR

Isn't that some title? When I saw this book, I was like, "Yes, ma'am. I'll take two." What I love about this book (and all of her other books) is that Valorie gives you quizzes, opportunities to journal throughout the book, and shares best practices for living a balanced life. If you are a recovering SBW (Strong Black Woman), then you need this book in your life...forever.

If You Have to Cry, Go Outside and Other Things Your Mother Never Told You.
Kelly Cutrone.
http://amzn.to/1O5ah64

I read her book before her stint as a judge on *America's Next Top Model*. This book is a must-read if you are still looking for your passion and purpose or if you need a gentle reminder. She also drops some serious science about being a WITCH (Woman In Total Control of Herself) at the workplace and in love.

Even though she isn't a sistergirl, her experience of overcoming internal and external obstacles is extremely relatable. After reading her advice, "We all have a tribe. Don't stop looking for yours," I called my college ex-boyfriend, who I realized I wanted in my life as a friend and not a lover, and told him that I was happy to have known him and wanted to keep in touch.

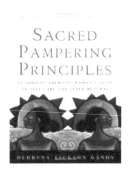

Sacred Pampering Principles: An African-American Woman's Guide to Self-care and Inner Renewal.
Debrena Jackson Gandy.
http://amzn.to/1FdiweW

I first read this book over 10 years ago because I was at the beginning of my quarter-life crisis and trying to figure this whole grown ass woman thing out. This book was extremely important to me as a black woman trying to let go of the need to be strong. Recently, I noticed the symptoms of dis-ease and put my nose back in that book to renew.

the frugalfeminista
financial empowerment. girl power. juicy living

Gentle Reminders for Recovering Strong Black Women

7 Adjectives That Accurately Describe Black Women

For years, one of my favorite lazy Saturday rituals was to go to my local thrift store and shop. On one particular Saturday I went in the afternoon and the radio was playing.

"Fellas, call in and tell me two things that you love about black women after the commercial break," the DJ said.

When I heard that question, my stomach immediately tightened. Even though I hadn't heard any of the listeners' perception of black women, I already knew (in my gut) what they were going to say.

"We're back. Caller, you on the line? What do you love about black women? What two qualities do you love about black women?"

"I love me a strong, independent black woman," the first black male caller responded.

By the time the third black responder said that same phrase, "strong black woman" I was in the coat section and in a bad mood.

"Why?" I asked myself, "are those the only damn words that come to mind when describing black women?"

I intellectually knew the answer— the intersection of race, class, and gender for black women in this country has meant having to reconcile a legacy of slavery and the creation of dehumanizing tropes and stereotypes like the Strong Black Woman (SBW), created by the white patriarchal engine to systemically control our reproduction, destroy our families, and distort how we saw ourselves and our men. And the truth is that black women had to be many things, one of which was strong, to endure the ravages of slavery and Jim Crow; I also understand that this is why we, as a culture, value this attribute at the expense of so many others.

But there is far more to being a black woman than being strong and independent. So, shortly after leaving the thrift store, I created my own survey and asked approximately 75 black women to describe themselves.

While I was disappointed to see that black women, too, had internalized many of the same stereotypes that have been paraded as truth, it was refreshing to see that many black women understood the complexity of their human experience and were able to articulate that complexity by choosing words that more fully and accurately encompass what it means to be a black woman.

Here are seven of the ways that black women surveyed see themselves that thankfully have nothing to do with being strong and/or independent:

1. **FASHIONABLE:** Some of us love to look good and smell good. We love to be on the cuttingedge of fashion trends. Others are always watching how we put colors together, how we attend to our hair, and how we attract the attention of others whenever we walk into a room.

2. **SPIRITUAL:** Black women describe themselves as women of faith whether they identify as Christian, Muslim, Rastafari, Santero, or "not religious, but spiritual". Black women strongly believe that they are connected to a higher being and that there is someone out there largerthan themselves.

3. **FAMILY-ORIENTED:** Black women are often the ones to remember the birthdays, send the Christmas cards, and plan the family reunions. Family fuels a lot of black women's happiness and sense of belonging.

4. **FUNNY:** Black women love to laugh and make their friends and families laugh. They push back against that ABW (Angry Black Woman) trope.

5. **HAPPY:** Similar to the concept of black women being funny, many sistergirls perceive black women as happy people with healthy emotional dispositions and worldviews. Their happiness also comes from their ability to be grateful.

6. **SEXY AND SENSUAL:** Black women embrace their sexuality and femininity. They feel desirable; they see the beauty of their skin tone, their features, their bodies, their natural smells, and their hair.

7. **INTELLIGENT:** Black women see themselves as cognitively well endowed. They believe that black women are able to juggle the matrix of life because of their ability to think quickly and creatively.

Language, words, labels. They all have the power to control our thinking, dictate how we treat others, and influence how we view ourselves.

It's up to us to reject the construct of the SBW when it brainwashes us into thinking that that is all that we are and nothing more. That we are without complexity, nuance, voice, or humanity.

4 Ways to Kill The "Strong Black Woman" Syndrome So You Can Be Happy Again

If I could quit my job, buy a pick-up truck with a megaphone attached, and spend the rest of my days shouting from the top of my lungs and paraphrase one of my favorite bell hooks quotes "Strength is not the ability to overcome, but endure," I would.

It is such an important concept for black families to understand—black women are not here to live their lives shouldering the burdens of others. Seriously. There has to be a point where we go beyond the act of enduring, silent suffering, and noble martyrdom. (That's for the birds.)

Black women, like any other women, are entitled to transformation, happiness, hope, and the full spectrum of their feminine humanity.

And celebrating the tired trope of black women's strength in our households clips our collective proverbial wings.

Give us free...

If you see the black women that you love running themselves ragged to hold everyone down and everything together as primary breadwinners and chief emotional caregivers in the family because of the unrealistic expectations placed on them, please help her by doing the following:

1.REMIND HER THAT HER WORTH IS NOT MEASURED BY WHAT SHE DOES FOR OTHERS, BUT BY WHO SHE IS. The black woman in your life should not have to prove herself worthy of love. Her presence, her support, and her decision to share her life with you should be enough. This doesn't mean that she shouldn't be allowed to do things for others, but if she is jeopardizing her health for the family, she needs to know that she is not helping anyone by neglecting herself.

2.SEND HER TO THE SPA OR THERAPY FOR MANDATORY PAMPERING AND SELF-CARE. Despite what it looks like from the outside, the typical "strong black woman" is a pile of nerves on the inside. She is often frazzled, anxious, and worried but does not feel that she can remove the mask and get her needs met. Sending her to a spa or therapy can be a soothing and rejuvenating practice that will help slow down life's pace so she can catch her breath in addition to letting her guard down to confide in someone for support and answers.

3.TEACH HER THE POWER OF "NO." SAYING "NO" SAVES LIVES. If you study the typical strong black woman, she may seem saucy and sassy and she may in fact have a few choice colorful words for you when you make an obscenely obnoxious request, but you rarely hear her say "no". Deep inside, your strong black woman is eager to please, believes in loyalty (to a fault), and somehow believes that saying no will destroy a relationship. She needs to know that the practice of saying "no" is important for creating personal boundaries, reducing feelings of resentment and burn-out, and strengthening others in the family to grow up and take the lead more often.

HIGHLIGHT HER OTHER POSITIVE QUALITIES. As a culture, we praise the attribute of strength in our black women. And it makes sense— up to a point. Because of our history in this country as slaves and second-class citizens, black women had to pull from a spiritual reserve and mental fortitude to make things work. But the black female experience is more than its history of marginalization and as a community, we need to focus on the qualities that round out black women's complete humanity.

Besides being strong, black women are funny, beautiful, generous, financially savvy, feminine, loyal, kind, creative, and a host of other things. I bet she would love to hear all of these things as well.

When was the last time you told her that?

the
frugalfeminista
financial empowerment. girl power. juicy living

Being Stronger Isn't Always a Good Thing... Or Is It?

When I was in graduate school studying bilingual education, I had to complete my student teaching in a school that was two and a half hours away from me on public transportation. I lived in Hollis, Queens and had to take one bus and two trains to get me to the school in the heart of Washington Heights.

And for the most part, I took my licks like every other commuter on New York City transit without complaint for most of the semester.

But that was until I awoke one morning writhing in such a devil pain. My behind and my mouth made at least a dozen sets of contact with the toilet seat that December morning and it wasn't even 6 a.m.

All I wanted to do was die right there on the bathroom floor. It would have saved me from having to deal with an immune system that had an agenda of its own.

My mother, though, a retired nurse for more than three years, was still an early riser. When she saw my face and heard my story, she told me that I should pull myself together, toughen up and make my way to Washington Heights. And by the looks of the clock on the cable box, I did not have much time to get ready.

Unlike any other student teaching day, that winter morning I was scheduled to do my final demonstration lesson of the semester. Just do it and be done, my mother said, then you can come home and rest.

the frugalfeminista
financial empowerment. girl power. juicy living

I did not agree with her logic but I obeyed nonetheless. She even paid for a taxi to the subway to cut down on my journey.

I wasn't lucky enough to get a seat near the window in the corner so I could tuck away and rest my increasingly sweaty head against the window. Instead, I was wedged in the middle of one of those F-train three seaters at 179th Street, the first and last stop of this train.

Through a series of stubborn swallows I managed to keep the vomit that yo-yoed up and down my throat like a milkshake in a straw in check. That was until we hit train traffic delays and my vomit couldn't contain itself. Right as we hit 50th Street, it started to gush past the blockade of my mouth like a wild mob breaking through a police barricade.

Although my main priority was to keep myself calm, I found myself distracted, apologizing in my head for the behavior of my messy insides-- how much space they might be taking up, how inconvenient it was for them to exist especially at such a busy time, and how rude of them for wanting to be released in public view.

When the train finally stopped at 50th Street and the doors opened, I was able to get off. Alone on the platform, I was able to continue to vomit; at least this time with some privacy and some dignity.

The funny thing about 50th street was that it was the figurative fork in the road. It was midway between my home and my destination: I could have crossed over to the other side of the train tracks and taken my brown sick body back to Queens and back to bed or I could have "fought the good fight" as I had been taught by the black women in my life.

I chose the latter.

I made it to the school on time and completed my final student teaching lesson flawlessly. In fact, I slayed it.

But that was the only part of my mother's plan that went off without a hitch. I asked to leave early once I completed my task, but I couldn't make it back home to Queens to rest because my body had shut down.

I was able to call a good friend that lived in Harlem to see if I could stop by and pass out. Luckily for me, he was home. For the rest of the day, I became as intimate and familiar with his toilet as I had done mine earlier that morning.

There is the saying that what does not kill you makes you stronger, but sometimes I have to wonder why death is the measuring stick and barometer for growth.

For whatever it is worth, I believe that I received an A as my final grade for the course. At least, I think I did.

BlackWomen'sLives Matter Too: A Tribute to Sybrina Fulton, Trayvon Martin's Mom

Since Trayvon Martin's death in 2012, his mother, Sybrina Fulton has been seen as a warrior in the #BlackLivesMatter movement. She has founded the Trayvon Martin Foundation, served as spiritual support to Black families, has spoken out at rallies, organized protests, and been relentless behind closed-door meetings fighting for justice for her son and other black men who have been killed unjustly.

On February 5th, the day that Trayvon would have turned twenty years old, she was asked how she was feeling on a television interview. I stopped what I was doing and turned up the volume. I wondered if she was willing to explicitly articulate, with her words, the visible weariness and acute sadness communicated in her eyes.

To paraphrase, she said that waking up on the morning that should have been her son's birthday was painful. She said that she wanted to stay in bed; on that day, nothing went right and she wished the day could have ended sooner.

I was relieved that Ms. Fulton seized this opportunity to express her full humanity. Equally important, I'm glad that America had a chance to see Ms. Fulton outside the caricature of the steely, strong, and fierce freedom fighter that we, as a nation have fully supported and embraced and should take responsibility in co-creating.

For black and white folk alike, the "black woman built outta brick" is part of our national identity and consciousness. Despite its empirical lack of veracity, we cling to this ideal during times of national crisis for a sense of collective comfort.

And yet.

Instead of dissembling and minimizing the pain of the death of her baby to stay strong for the movement, Ms. Fulton stood firm in her vulnerability and reminded the world that she is complex, human, and with every right to be seen as such.

I hope this act of public self-defining and self-healing is not overlooked. In a nation, where the intersection of race, gender, class, and policy, create heavy, unbearable realities for many black women to shoulder; and where we are asked to bury our pain and endure (preferably in silence), Sybrina Fulton, in stating that she was not okay, was asking more of herself, more of her community, and more of her country.

We need more of this.

Recently, Justice Ginsburg was interviewed and asked her thoughts about the success of the women's rights movement. Justice Ginsburg chronicled the various waves of triumph that women have achieved through the struggles of the movement: more equal wages, reproductive rights, and the dismantling of widespread stereotypical views around women working outside of the home.

And while these are wins, albeit uneven, and in favor of white women and women with means or access to capital, I would have to agree with Justice Ginsburg when she argued that the next wave of feminist work lies in fighting unconscious bias.

As black women continue to serve as the backbone of our homes, faith-based organizations, and communities; and as they strive to create a new sense of normalcy with arguably fewer emotional and financial resources in the midst of tragedy, it is important that we stop and remind ourselves that, like the black male lives lost unfairly to violence, the black lives of the black women who are left behind to hold things down and keep things together also matter; how well these black women attend to their feelings also matters; and how we fight against the distorted and limited beliefs that black women facing ungodly levels of suffering can toil without tears or strive without a stumble also matters.

When we replace oppressive beliefs and expectations around black women's inexhaustible strength and capability with more accurate and robust understandings of our complex humanity, we not only honor ourselves, but we also teach our daughters and others to do the same.

Bonus Resources

If reading *Unmasking The Strong Black Woman: 16 Essays on How to Manage Your Emotional Health, Build Your Wealth, and Live a Juicy Life* is leaving you wanting for more, then let me not stand in the way of your growth and personal development.

As a bonus for you, here are titles to five more essays written by members of The Frugal Feminista team and the larger black female global community. These are my top picks for further reading.

▸ If You Don't Allow Yourself to Feel, You're Going to Die: An Open Letter to The Strong Black Woman by Dr. Norissa Williams

▸ 3 Signs It's Time to Get Some Therapy by Christina Lattimore

▸ Bow Down, B*tches: Why It's Healthy and Essential to Embrace Our Internal Bitch by Dr. Norissa Williams

▸ 3 Tips to Handle Discouragement in a Healthy Way by Kim Renee Nelson

▸ Mammy, Jezebel, Sapphire and Their Homegirls: Developing an "Oppositional Gaze" Toward the Image of Black Women by Dr. Carolyn M. West

http://www.thefrugalfeminista.com/

A Final Note From Kara

"The most common way people give up their power is by thinking they don't have any." -Alice Walker

You've reached the end of *Unmasking The Strong Black Woman: 16 Essays on How to Manage Your Emotional Health, Build Your Wealth, and Live a Juicy Life*. All you have left to do is show the world the woman behind your mask.

Prior to this read, you may have found it difficult to self-describe without using the word "strong." I hope that now your joy, your self-love, and your financial savvy will outshine that "strong-only" mask.

Please let me know how your journey goes. Let's keep in touch via email at kara@thefrugalfeminista.com or via Twitter @frugalfeminista

Love,

Kara

CPSIA information can be obtained
at www.ICGtesting.com
Printed in the USA
LVHW071810130720
660547LV00001B/11